NAVEGADOR SERIES℠

Reignite

Principles to light your heart and mind on fire

DR. ANITZA SAN MIGUEL

NAVEGADOR SERIES^{SM}

NAVEGADOR SERIES: Reignite

© Copyright 2023, Dr. Anitza San Miguel.
All rights reserved.

No portion of this book may be reproduced by mechanical, photographic or electronic process, nor may it be stored in a retrieval system, transmitted in any form or otherwise be copied for public use or private use without written permission of the copyright owner.

It is sold with the understanding that the publisher and the individual author are not engaged in the rendering of psychological, legal, accounting or other professional advice. The content and views in each chapter are the sole expression and opinion of the author and not necessarily the views of Fig Factor Media, LLC.

Cover Design by Marco Alvarez
Layout by LDG Juan Manuel Serna Rosales

Printed in the United States of America

ISBN: 978-1-959989-29-5
Library of Congress Control Number: 2023906948

Scripture quotations taken from The Holy Bible, New International Version®, NIV®. Copyright© 1973, 1978, 1984, 2011 by Biblica, Inc.®
Used by permission. All rights reserved worldwide.

NAVEGADOR SERIES℠

I dedicate this book series to all of my spiritual mentors who have guided me throughout my life. You are all my inspiration. I have learned from each of you that without God in my life and without seeking His guidance and direction, my life would not be the same. Thank you! It is because of God's grace that I am where I am. It is because of you and your continuous support and prayers that have lifted me in my darkest moments.

NAVEGADOR SERIES℠

TABLE OF CONTENTS

Acknowledgments 5

Introduction 6

    REIGNITE 8

    RENEWAL 10

    SEEK 12

    SPEAK 14

    VALUE 16

    TRANSFORM 18

    BELIEVE 20

    EQUIP 22

    PROCESS 24

    GO 26

    REKINDLE 28

    COMMITMENT 30

About the Author 32

ACKNOWLEDGMENTS

A special thank you to my mentor and friend, Jacqueline Ruiz. Thank you for believing in me and seeing the *"magix"* within me. Thank you for helping me build my legacy.

Also, a special thank you to my husband, Juan M. Morales. Thank you for all of your support and encouragement as I navigate this journey of entrepreneurship.

Thank you to my daughter, Andrea I. Morales, for listening and understanding mommy. You are special to me and God.

NAVEGADOR SERIES℠

INTRODUCTION

When God puts an idea in my mind and heart, I listen and I take action. This book series was born of my personal and spiritual growth journey. Since the day "Navegador" was born, I knew I was embarking on a journey where my vision wasn't clear. What I have learned in the process is that time will teach me the lessons that I need to know. Time has taught me to wait on the Lord. God has not shown me exactly what I will find on my journey, but has equipped me for the journey. I am qualified for the work He has called me to do. I don't have the whole vision, but He is my guide. He is the lighthouse that illuminates my path.

My purpose is that this book, as other books in the Navegador Series, will serve you as a guide to reignite the passion and potential that is in you, so you can grow and shine your unique light. If I did it, so can you. Everything is possible if you trust, believe, and take action.

Other books in this series are Grow and Shine.

Blessings!

NAVEGADOR SERIES℠

NAVEGADOR SERIES℠

Reignite

"For this reason I remind you to fan into flame the gift of God, which is in you through the laying on of my hands."
2 Timothy 1:6

When I think about the word reignite, I think about increasing the flame, desire, passion, and potential that is in me. Challenges and life circumstances may dim my flame, but when I plug in to God's word, the flame comes back to life.

Renewal

But those who hope in the Lord will renew their strength. They will soar on wings like eagles; they will run and not grow weary, they will walk and not be faint."

Isaiah 40:31

Renew your thoughts. Focus on the positive. The limiting beliefs are going to show up when you least expect it. Acknowledge the thought and shut it down by creating a positive thought. It can be as simple as adding the word "yet." Instead of saying "I can't do it," say "I'm unable to do this at this time, yet. I know I can and I will do it. I trust myself, my talents and abilities." Always remember that many things in life require practice and patience.

NAVEGADOR SERIES℠

Seek

"Look to the Lord and his strength; seek his face always."
Psalms 105:4

I grew up in the church in my hometown of Toa Baja, Puerto Rico. As a teenager, I led a small kids' group during Sunday school and Summer. Growing up in church doesn't automatically mean that you have experience with God. It was not until recently that I intentionally started seeking God. I now intentionally seek His guidance and to be in His presence. As you navigate, seek opportunities that elevate you. Seek His presence.

NAVEGADOR SERIES℠

Speak

Do not be afraid; keep on speaking, do not be silent. For I am with you, and no one is going to attack and harm you, because I have many people in this city." *Acts 18:9-10*

Speak from your heart. Silence the doubts. Conquer your fears.

As I soar to new levels, I have learned to be quick to hear and slow to speak. Fear, lack of confidence, lack of self-esteem, and not knowing my value kept me from speaking up. Once I recognized my value and what God created me for, I found my purpose and started to speak freely.

NAVEGADOR SERIES℠

Value

VALUE

Look at the birds of the air; they do not sow or reap or store away in barns, and yet your heavenly Father feeds them. Are you not much more valuable than they?"
Matthew 6:26

I am unique. I am a precious pearl. I was created with a purpose. I am loved. I am brave. I am valuable. You were created with a purpose. God has created you with a unique image and that makes you valuable. Never forget it, YOU ARE VALUABLE!

NAVEGADOR SERIES℠

Transform

"Do not conform to the pattern of this world, but be transformed by the renewing of your mind. Then you will be able to test and approve what God's will is – his good, pleasing and perfect will." *Romans 12:2*

Over the last four years, I have seen my own transformation. When I started my intentional growth journey, I realized that the first thing I needed to do was to transform my thoughts. I needed to reprogram my mind to think differently.

Transforming your thoughts is the first step to reprogramming your mind. In His word, God calls us to transform our life by the renewal of our mind; our understanding. Many times, we want change, but we are not willing to make the journey. We want the benefits that transforming and renewing our minds brings, but we are not willing to do the work.

NAVEGADOR SERIES℠

Believe

YOU WILL MAKE IT BECAUSE THE LORD IS ON YOUR SIDE.

So do not fear, for I am with you; do not be dismayed, for I am your God. I will strengthen you and help you; I will uphold you with my righteous right hand." *Isaiah 41:10*

Believe in you. Believe in your talents, skills, and abilities. Believe that the Creator God is with you and in you at all times. Believe that he can do the impossible. Believe!

NAVEGADOR SERIES℠

Equip

>
> So Christ himself gave the apostles, the prophets, the evangelists, the pastors, and teachers, to equip his people for works of service, so that the body of Christ may be built up." *Ephesians 4:11-12*

God will not give you what you are not equipped to undertake. The challenges that you are facing now equip you for the next level. Trust the process. While you wait, prepare. Take the time to equip yourself.

Process

Being confident of this, that he who began a good work in you will carry it on to completion until the day of Christ Jesus." *Philippians 1:6*

That challenge you are living now is a process. A process that you and only you have to live. We want all of the benefits but we don't want to go through the process. It is through the process that we grow and learn. God is with you every step of the way. Trust Him. He is working behind the scenes.

NAVEGADOR SERIES℠

Go

The Lord our God said to us at Horeb, 'You have stayed long enough at this mountain. Break camp and advance into the hill country of the Amorites.'" *Deuteronomy 1:6-7a*

It's time for you to move out of your comfort zone. You have been too comfortable waiting to see what happens. You have been a spectator for too long. It's time for you to work for your dreams, goals, and desires. Four years ago, I moved out of my comfort zone. I was very comfortable doing what was familiar. It's time to break the cycle. Go! God is calling you.

NAVEGADOR SERIES℠

Rekindle

For this reason I remind you to fan into flame the gift of God, which is in you through the laying on of my hands. For the Spirit God gave us does not make us timid, but gives us power, love and self-discipline." *2 Timothy 1:6-7*

Rekindle your purpose and your potential. God created you with a purpose. You have all you need to take action. Rekindle the gifts that God gave you. Don't let fear, anxiety, and people's opinion rob you of what is yours. It's time to take control of you and navigate in the direction of your dreams.

NAVEGADOR SERIES℠

Commitment

COMMITMENT

Commit your way to the Lord; trust in him and he will do this." *Psalms 37:5*

Commit yourself to be you. You don't have to be what others want you to be. Do you. Be you. Commit to your personal (and spiritual) growth and development. If you don't do it, no one will do it for you.

ABOUT THE AUTHOR

Dr. Anitza San Miguel is wife, mom, scientist, educator, and transformational leadership coach. Her purpose is to help leaders reignite the potential and passion within them, so they can grow and shine their unique light, transform their mind, and unleash their potential to create their best version without limits.

Her passion for personal growth and development drives her to grow daily. She has more than twenty years of experience in research and education. She has served as a science professor and dean of science at institutions in Virginia and Florida, and currently serves as a dean leading a team in the Orlando, Florida area. She worked at the National Institutes of Health (NIH) and the United States Patent and Trademark Office (USPTO).

She is also the founder of ASM Mentors, creator of the podcast "Sacúdete y Toma Acción" translated in English as "Shake It Off and Take Action." Dr. San Miguel has

ABOUT THE AUTHOR

been showcased in numerous platforms in social media, and other events, including TV programs in Puerto Rico. She authored *Navegador,* a reflective journaling tool with reflection cards, and was featured as an insightful author in *Today's Inspired Latina Volume X* and *Today's Inspired Leader Volume IV* book series. She is also a sought-after speaker, mentor, and coach.

Dr. San Miguel firmly believes that everything is possible if you trust, believe, and take action. Her attitude, positive energy, and determination have led her to achieve her professional and personal goals.

When she's not working, you'll find her spending quality time with her husband and fourteen-year-old daughter, traveling, and journaling.

She is passionate about education that leads to the academic and professional success of leaders with the mission of discovering their best version without limits.

DR. ANITZA SAN MIGUEL
anitza@anitzasanmiguel.com
LinkedIn: /anitza-sanmiguel
Instagram: @anitza21
anitzasanmiguel.com

To view Dr. Anitza San Miguel's other books, please visit: anitzasanmiguel.com.

NAVEGADOR SERIESᴿᴹ

www.ingramcontent.com/pod-product-compliance
Lightning Source LLC
Chambersburg PA
CBHW041415010526
44107CB00016B/1172